IS YOUR FAMILY TURNED ON?

Coping with the Drug Culture

Other books by Charlie W. Shedd

PROMISES TO PETER: BUILDING A BRIDGE FROM PARENT TO CHILD

THE STORK IS DEAD

LETTERS TO PHILIP: ON HOW TO TREAT A WOMAN

LETTERS TO KAREN: ON KEEPING LOVE IN MARRIAGE

PASTORAL MINISTRY OF CHURCH OFFICERS

HOW TO DEVELOP A PRAYING CHURCH

TIME FOR ALL THINGS

HOW TO DEVELOP A TITHING CHURCH

IS YOUR FAMILY TURNED ON?

Coping with the Drug Culture

CHARLIE W. SHEDD

WORD BOOKS,
PUBLISHER
Waco, Texas

IS YOUR FAMILY TURNED ON?

For information, write Word Books, Publisher,
Waco, Texas 76703.

Library of Congress Catalog Card Number: 71-165959

Printed in the United States of America

To Paul

and millions of others—

cool young thinkers

too many to count—

Dynamic youth

on a natural high

CONTENTS

Fifty winners were chosen from the thousands of entries in our "Why I Don't Use Drugs" contest. Pertinent quotations from their entries are an integral part of this book.

The top twenty winners are pictured. Interestingly, three of them were raised by "single" parents. It is encouraging that mothers or fathers faced with this particular problem can effectively fill the place of both parents.

Help on handling this complex relationship is found in Chapter 12, "The Parent Alone," PROMISES TO PETER, by Charlie W. Shedd.

THE ONE SAFE PLACE

THE ONE SAFE PLACE

"Do you know any place where my kids would be safe from drugs? If I only knew one place! I'd give up my job and we'd move. I mean anywhere in the country. No matter what it cost that's where we'd go. Is there any place like that?"

It was plain he wasn't kidding. He had been reading one of those articles by a torn-up parent. You know the kind. Father, excellent writer, describes his heartache for drug-addict son. Honor student. Never a moment's trouble. Then before anyone knew what happened—total behavior change. Awesome.

So he turned to me and asked it from way down inside. We were sitting together 30,000 feet up, total strangers.

Of course, we introduced ourselves and discovered a lot in common. I have five children too. He told me about his job—lead engineer, electronics. I told him about mine. I work with teenagers. He travels a lot. So do I.

And I had to admit I couldn't tell him one place safe from drugs.

But I found one.

****

We were having breakfast at a restaurant in Houston, Texas. This was a group of my favorite people. They meet together regularly and some of my best ideas come from this source. What I got that day was one line from Paul.

Paul is a college senior. If you could see him, you would say, "Good." Tall. Handsome. Cool. The kind who doesn't say much. But when he does, you listen.

We were discussing the increasing use of narcotics. Then somebody asked Paul, "How come you haven't tried the drug thing?"

He thought a while as he is prone to do. Then he came with this:

> "Every morning I get up wondering what exciting thing is going to happen today. Most of the ones who go on dope are bored. I'm not. I believe life is already coming at me with enough good things if I just stay ready."

I went away from that breakfast determined to ask some others, "How come you haven't gone the drug route?" I asked it in big cities and small towns; in ghettos and fashionable suburbs. In colleges and universities, in high schools and junior highs, in coffee houses, seminars, classrooms, assemblies. Everywhere, I asked it. Always the same, it checked out:

> THE ONE PLACE SAFE FROM DRUGS IS A MIND AND HEART WHICH HAS DECIDED IT DOESN'T NEED THEM.

****

There are millions who have made this decision. Drugs aren't for them. But the tendency is to miss that fact. Which is no new thing as my philosophy professor knew—

"Tell me quick: What do you see?"

That's how he started his class this day. Holding up the large white cardboard, he asked his question. And we all saw one thing: a blob of black ink.

He did it every year in his classes, and he said it was always the same. It took some time before anyone said, "I see a big white cardboard." For one spot of black, we missed all that white.

It is something like this with the drug scene. For some reason the bizarre claims our attention. Now and then the nonusers get some publicity, but not much. Generally the main note is on the down beat.

This is too bad, because it is a fact that there are many more who don't than do. Hundreds, thousands, millions of young people are not on narcotics and do not plan to be.

Yet anyone who can see or hear or think knows it for grim truth: We are faced with a problem of catastrophic proportions. Rose-colored glasses we do not need. Nor Pollyannas. Somebody has to deal with this monster. And unless we can get the job done we are headed for the dump heap. History shows us clearly that life can only stand so much of the unreal. It's as though the universe finally becomes angry at those who insult it with artificial stimulants.

So what's the answer?

I think I found this too.

A short time after that breakfast in Houston, I was in California on a television show. We were interviewing some addicts. They came from one of the fine West Coast recovery centers. Our theme for this day was, "Why?"

Nothing unusual about that. Anyone who works the teen scene has been down this road, looking for answers.

But so many times the user doesn't know why. He's looking for answers too. His reasons can only be a mixture of gray fact and distortion.

So that day as I listened to their fuzzy answers, I thought of Paul. I thought of hundreds like him who have turned their backs to the pusher. What would they say if we asked them their reasons? And as I mused on these things, I thought to myself, "We're talking to the wrong crowd. We need to be asking the young whose heads are still clear: 'How come you're ***not*** on drugs?' "

****

So my publisher and I decided to tap the reservoir of these great young citizens. We would have a contest.

We offered some attractive prizes for the best 250-word statements on WHY I DON'T USE DRUGS.

To every sector of the country we sent our WHY I DON'T USE DRUGS poster. It went to public and private schools, high schools and junior highs.

It went to small colleges and large universities. One thousand of them went to little towns and sprawling urban centers; to pockets of poverty and places of affluence. West Coast, East Coast, Midwest, North, South. Every racial background. Every color, every class.

On first announcement, we offered a single

WHY I DON'T USE DRUGS

five hundred dollar prize. But because of the amazing response and high quality, we altered our plans. Raising cash prizes to two thousand, we decided to conduct our study from a broader base.

Judges were thirty people under thirty. These too came from a wide selection by age and geography.

When prizes had been awarded, we began to research what the winners were saying. Noting particular statements, we wrote them for more information:

"Where did you get these ideas you express so well?"

"How did you come by the principles which have made you what you are?"

"What shaped you?"

In some cases we wrote their parents.

Wherever we could, my publisher and I have met the winners personally. To put it mildly, this has been some kind of special thrill. Anyone of low morale would take courage. Given youth of this caliber in sufficient number, mankind's future has to be good.

Throughout the book when we quote from the fifty winners, we give their names. Other quotes are from additional entries; from discussion groups and seminars; or from extensive correspondence in connection with this book and THE STORK IS DEAD.*

The statements of our fifty winners are unbelievable for their beauty. And no small part of their beauty is in their logic. They not only have strong feelings about why they aren't on drugs, they also know what has shaped them.

And the conclusion won't have it any other way—there is only one place safe from drugs.

So, let's go on curing the addict. He needs every help we can give him.

Let's improve drug laws. A people with no laws would soon be animals running amuck.

Let's do whatever we can to nail the pusher. He cares for no one. He finances his problem by creating another problem. He floats in and out. His tracks are almost impossible to trace. But we better keep trying.

Let's go for drug centers and research.

Let's hope for new medicines, new approaches.

---

*Editor's note: In connection with the publication of his book, THE STORK IS DEAD (Waco, Texas: Word Books, 1968), Dr. Shedd has received more than 25,000 letters from teenagers. In addition, he talks with thousands of young people every year in church- and civic-sponsored Parent-Teen seminars throughout the U.S. FWT

Anything that works. We need it.

But, no matter how effective, these are not the final answer. There has to be something better than cleaning up the debris and solving the problem at its edges.

What we need more than anything else is a new generation. The final answer is homes where young hearts are turned on early. Turned on to the beauties of self and other people and the world around them.

And this kind of heart is the one safe place.

CONTRAST

What are the major differences between user and nonuser? We asked ourselves this, as we combed our entries. Already, from many sources, we had a composite of the user.* Would some common traits show up in our winners' statements? They did. Actually, there are almost as many subtle variations as there are teenagers. But the overall contrast looks like this.

The user has a negative recall of his family background.

The user needs artificial stimulation for his turned-off responses.

The user feels that life has not done right by him.

*Throughout this book the term "user" applies to those who indulge themselves with drugs. The percentage of those who have tried various drugs (mostly marijuana) would shock many adults. Isolated episodes of trying grass do ***not*** label a young person "user." But the growing number who are overindulging is cause for alarm.

1. ***The nonuser*** thinks back to his home with warm feelings of togetherness.

2. ***The nonuser*** comes at his day with anticipation.

3. ***The nonuser*** is appreciative.

The user has a low self-estimate which makes him cynical.

The user does not experience the thrill of accomplishment.

The user tends to fold when life goes against him.

The user cares little for his country and the law.

The user is sexually immature, making him confused about his role.

The user struggles to be free, and his feelings of repression make him hostile.

The user suffers from chronic despair because he has little faith in anything.

4. ***The nonuser*** has a healthy attitude toward himself.

5. ***The nonuser*** knows the satisfaction of work well done.

6. ***The nonuser*** faces the hard things with courage.

7. ***The nonuser*** is preparing himself for responsible citizenship.

8. ***The nonuser*** respects his sexuality, so he is not afraid to be male or female.

9. ***The nonuser*** has been encouraged to use his own judgment, giving him a healthy independence.

10. ***The nonuser*** feels responsible to God and he is grateful to Him.

I

"I FEEL BLENDED ENOUGH ALREADY"

The nonuser thinks back to his home with warm feelings of togetherness

The user has a negative recall of his family background

I "I FEEL BLENDED ENOUGH ALREADY"

FAMILY TOGETHERNESS

> "There is this boy at our school who is a pusher. He keeps trying to get me to take some of his grass free. You know why he does that, don't you? He keeps saying, 'Here, this stuff will really make you blend.' I keep telling him, 'But, Frank, I fell blended enough already.'"
>
> From a Pennsylvania high school senior

Ask a user his reason, one of the most common explanations has to do with his desire to belong. This is true of some of the marijuana crowd. And even more of those on the hard stuff.

Frequently, they tell me: "I guess what my friends and I like most about it is how it melts us together . . . . I feel like all the people in the world are one. No color lines, no class lines. Everybody the same. You know what I mean? This sensation that we are all together, it's beautiful."

Most of the drug users I know are not satisfied with their present relationships. Some-

Jody Caudill—that All-American girl next door—brilliant mind with every brain turning over, turning on to life—is one more product of a home where roads are open to people and things.

"I think the drug problem in Aspen High is largely due to the many broken homes and unhappy family situations, as well as the social need to be a part of the crowd. Being an individual is difficult, for there exists that need for a sense of belonging. I have a very close family, therefore giving me security."

thing in them, something between them and other people speaks of crevices—sometimes chasms. What happened to create the fissure? What didn't happen that the gaps were left open?

> "One night I went to this party where everyone was turning on. But there were two of my friends who didn't. So we just sat back and listened. Have you ever heard what people say when they are turning on? It's hard to follow sometimes, but sometimes you listen and you know what is bugging them. This night they were all talking about belonging. Most of my friends who are taking drugs are lonesome. Maybe the reason why I don't is because I don't feel that way."
>
> College sophomore

The major common denominator among our winners is a feeling of closeness in the family circle! When does this begin? Apparently very early, but this is for sure: the earlier it starts in the child's heart, the better.

Principle: The sooner we can create a feeling of family togetherness, the longer we can make it last, plus, the deeper we can make it go; the better our chances for healthy emotions and strong character.

****

DRUGS AS A SUBSTITUTE FOR LOVE

When
we realize the pressures young people are getting to join the users . . .

When
we understand that pushers are looking for dollars and the hooked are frantically creating new customers to support their habit . . .

When
we know how desperate the users are for companionship, love, friends, for anybody who will share anything with them . . .

When
we understand that some of our children's friends want to gain another user to justify their own usage . . .

When
we can grasp all this, we will know how important this solid base of home and family togetherness can be.

We have done a great thing when we have provided our children this powerful antidote to peer pressures.

CHILDREN OF THE FUTURE

Comes now one of the most beautiful refrains from our winners' statements. This generation is taking a long look down the road ahead to their own children, even to their grandchildren.

Sue Ballard Hilton was single and a college senior at the time of the contest. Now married, she says: "The decision we made not to use drugs is one we made together."

"I do not use drugs or hallucinogens because not enough is known about their long-range effects. Coming from a family of five and being the oldest, I guess I've always been involved with the idea of having babies. I won't take any risk that might hinder my having healthy, normal children. • The young people who take drugs today may not see deformities or deficiencies in their own children, but it may appear in their grandchildren. My fiance and I have talked about this, and we feel that our children will have a head start because we never experimented with drugs."

To which a chorus of echoes:

"I really love life and
one day I want very much to
get married and have children.
My future children have more
right to normal births and
lives than I shall ever
have to take drugs."

Valentine
Chong

"I am in love with
the future, and what it
holds for me. I can see
dozens of happy,
healthy, beautiful children,
running and growing up.
They won't have to worry
about defects, retardation,
or sickness, because they
are all whole and perfect.
I, as their grandmother,
look back . . . .
glad that I didn't
use drugs."

Mary Hightower

"One of the biggest
reasons
for not using drugs is
that I want to be able to
enjoy my grandchildren
and enjoy life
to its fullest."

Dave Massey

"It is wrong
to place
any children I
might have
in danger."

Karen Morris

"In some cases,
LSD has caused a mutation
in the chromosomes
and therefore caused the
babies to be deformed.
Is a trip on LSD worth the
enjoyment one might miss
in having his children
grow up healthy and
happy?"

Melissa Thompson

"I want to some day bear
beautiful children,
not deformed ones whose chances of
a normal healthy life
are ruined even before they're born.
Such potent drugs as young people
are experimenting with today
upset all their body metabolisms,
including their childbearing
systems."

Carol Warner

Check out the young lady standing by the nursery window, looking at those newborn babies. Chances are she is dreaming of her own family-to-come. There is a glow in her soul as she looks forward. But it probably had its start out of warm recall from her own family. True, there are those who feel this way because they want to make up for lost time. They didn't have it and they hope their children will. But most of us are put together like this—we want to pass on to others the good things we have experienced.

****

Valentine Chong
is a
Georgia high schooler.
Popular. Plenty of
boy friends. But
thinking into the
distance.

"My parents take
all the time they
can with me. They try to
give me good advice and
answers to my problems.
I hope when I become a parent
I can be as good a parent
as my parents have been."

There isn't a thinking parent who wouldn't like to have this said about him. So how do we create these feelings? Some clear answers come from our winners.

First, that child will most respect his parent, whose parent respects his individuality. This is so important for keeping the roads open at home we will give a whole section to it later.

A second quality which produces respect is honesty. The thrust here is not honesty from parent to child about the child; it is rather the parent's honesty about himself. The healthiest parent-child atmosphere follows this line: "We are not perfect parents. We make mistakes.

"Some moms and dads never will admit they're wrong. One thing I like about my folks is that they will apologize sometimes. This helps a lot because you listen more to people like that."

Seventh grader

Every decision we make won't be wise and every action right. There will be times when you won't like us, because we're not likable. But we want to do better and you can help us. Whenever we're unbearable, whenever you find us at less than our best, tell us. You try to bring it to us in a nice way and we'll try to be nice about talking it over." There is something so beautifully respectable about knowing where we aren't what we should be.

Warning: The parent who demands respect must understand that respect is not to be had on demand. This stuff is earned, not forced.

We have already seen that the happiest child is not one who is given all he wants of material things. The same thing holds for regulations. That parent who insists on certain standards is more likely to be respected. Security comes in part from well-defined limits.

Most young people don't look to their mom and dad for a "pal" relationship. They resent any kind of phoney hypertogetherness. Some of the drug users I know come from a smothering background. The child-parent feeling is much more than "buddy-buddy." Our children want parents who are friends—the kind of friends who will contain them, guide them, love them with a productive kind of discipline.

LISTENING PARENTS

Steve Bartholomew is a high schooler from one of the nation's largest cities. Like so many of our winners, his parent-thoughts are strong to the positive side.

"Young people who use drugs are trying to get away from their problem. But the problem becomes bigger the more they depend on drugs. They will keep doing this until someone helps them. If I had a problem, I would go to my parents. Why would I go to them? I would go to my parents because I can depend on them to listen. Some young people don't think their parents would try to see it their way. So they find some other way. The only way some know to try is drugs. So that is why I don't use drugs. My parents listen to me and so I know they love me."

This is another steady beat from the non-user. He's being heard. And that is not all. He knows he won't always win, but he will be listened to. What he says is received with respect. He feels the dignity of his own opinions. His judgment counts.

In too many homes this is not true.

> "Why I don't ever go to my parents is they hear my words, but not what I'm saying. They already have their minds made up and they can't see it any other way. So, why should I bother?"

Good question!

There is only one answer:

He shouldn't bother. To dialogue with parents like this is a waste of time.

There are not many things more appreciated by the growing youngsters than these:

(a) time spent together;

(b) the assurance that he will be heard.

For twelve years old,
Anastasia Thomopoulos is
some kind of special.
Los Angeles, California,
her home town, is a
challenging place for parents
to raise children.
Her mother and father
obviously know
what they are doing.

"Everything in our home is based on one element, understanding. We love one another and are open with each other. The way I am taught right from wrong is not by rules. I am told why it isn't proper and why I shouldn't do it. My mom and dad are not only mom and dad, but my friends. Knowing they want to help and share problems and ideas, that's what counts.

II

SONGBIRDS AND SAUSAGES

The nonuser comes at his day with anticipation

The user needs artificial stimulation for his turned-off responses

II SONGBIRDS AND SAUSAGES

Becky Bavin is a college junior. Alert to the world around her, she lives with a song in her heart. Indoors her interests run to domestic things—cooking, sewing, knitting. Outdoors, she likes hiking and horseback. Our judges awarded her a second place tie for $250.

"Why don't I use drugs? Life simply has too much to offer. Why should I be willing to sacrifice my life for a fleeting moment of artificial exhilaration? Why should I want to escape from a world in which I can find the delicacy and grace of a flower, the sincerity and innocence of a child, or the sun-blushed splendor of the afternoon desert? • My parents have undoubtedly been the strongest influence in my life. It was through their eyes that I first saw the wonders of my world. They pointed out the magic of life until I could finally see it for myself. They taught me early to do my part to make the world run by hard work, honesty, love, family chores, social duties, responsibility and discipline, the sister of responsibility. As love was given freely to me, I learned to give it to others and the rewards have been beyond belief. The more love that flows out from my heart, the more joy I find. • My Creator has given me life and an ever changing marvelous world to live it in. Today I stop to listen to the songbird. Tomorrow promises thrills unmeasurable as I look forward to learning and living in God's wild, wonderful world."

A Montana prison chaplain, worker with the young in jails and penitentiaries, widely experienced with drug users in and out of prison, says: "When parents ask me, 'What can we do to keep our kids off dope?' I answer with two words, 'Be happy!' "

This has to be right on target, if we believe our entries. "Life is good" . . . "I celebrate every day just being alive" . . . "Already there is this great song in my heart" . . . "I don't need artificial stimulation. There are enough things revving me up without that" . . . "My life is too great to spoil it with drugs" . . . "The group I run with is so much fun. I think they feel like I do. Who needs it?" . . . "You know how it is with dope. Some of it peps you up. Some of it slows you down. Me? I feel like I got just the right amount of revolutions now" . . .

Reading the entries another thing comes clear. This crowd isn't parroting some phoney happiness. Their smiles are not cheesecake. These are the "I'm ***really*** glad I'm alive" people.

One more time: Happiness is a by-product. We create future misery for our children when we give them everything they want. When we overdo giving them ***things,*** we insinuate that life's deepest needs can be satis-

Vivacious
and thinking all
the time—that's
Jeannette Bolte.
A high school senior,
her life is filled
with exciting realities
and wonderful dreams.

" 'Naturally high!' Yes, that is a very nice term. It represents all the fantastic things that can turn me on; turned on by people and love. I live naturally stoned and I wouldn't have it any other way.
A natural high is a challenge. I am able to achieve it only because I have taken the time to decide what it is in life I value most. Then I must condition my mind to let happiness flow—uninhibited happiness.
The human mind is capable of achieving such a total high."

fied with material stuff. These "artificial stimulants" feed the appetite for artificial stimulants, which is what drugs are all about.

Quote from THE STORK IS DEAD correspondence:

> "I hope you won't mind me saying this, but honest I hate my mom. I mean I really do. Isn't that awful? But you said to tell you whatever we think. So that's what I think, and I can't figure it out. She always gave me everything I wanted. She even gave me a lot of things I didn't want. So why do I feel this way?"

By teaching them how to dream, to plan, how to get things for themselves, to earn, how to make things—we give them tools by which they can create their own happiness.* Always, long-range happiness is a trailer to more important things!

Question: Why do we want to give our children so much?

Is it partially to prove that we are good

---

*See PROMISES TO PETER. "The Joy Is in Deserving," pp. 140-44.

parents? Is it because material gifts are easier to give? Time, understanding, study of the deeper needs—these require more from us than things.

Thank God, many young people today are catching on.

> "You should see our home. Beautiful, man, beautiful. Swimming pool. The works. Then I began to groove on all this and I decided something. My father knocked himself out for it. You know, travel, worry, ulcers, Vice-Prez, the whole drag. But there was this one minor thing he overlooked. He never had time to enjoy it. Not me. When I get a kid, I'm going to have some fun with him."

****

ANTICIPATION

As I read the souls of the "turned-on-to-life" youth, their forward look has a double thrust. They are turned on for this day. They are also turned on to the days ahead.

This moves up front quickly in our entries. These are the "high expectancy" folks. They live on tiptoe waiting for what life offers next.

Patricia Popham is an Oklahoma college freshman, recipient of many honors; tennis player; and to borrow one of her own terms, "grooved on life."

Is there something in the world
I haven't learned?
I wish to realize it.

Is there color in skies
That I've missed, blinded by clouds?
I wish to see it.

Is there a gentleness in the ocean water
That I've left unnoticed?
I want to touch it.

Is there a tinge of sadness in children's laughter
That I've thoughtlessly disregarded?
I wish to know it.

Is there love and pain in love
That I have never experienced?
I want to feel it.

Is there a new idea
I may have let pass by?
I want to recall it.

Is there another depth of meaning to 'I love you'
That I cannot yet have known?
I want to understand it.

Are there thoughts of peace and God
That I have easily ignored?
I want to hear them.

Are there words being left unspoken
That I've let drown in ignorant silence?
I wish to voice them.

Are there songs lying still in my mind
That I have not yet discovered?
I wish to sing them.

Are there hands searching for help
That I have left unaided?
I want to reach them.

Are there dreams of my future
I have not yet explored?
I want to dream them.

Are there new and winding roads
That I have never walked?
I want to find them.

So I find the process of living
A beautiful experience
Of all the things I am;
Of all I want to be;
Of all I hope I can be.

This is why I don't take drugs.

STIMULATION OF INTERESTS

The nonuser is likely to have many things going for him. Somehow life itself has plenty of stimulants to pique his interest. On the other hand, boredom is another major cause of drug use. So, the more we can make life a mind-expanding business, the less need there will be for artificial mind-expanders.

Tap one of our contestants on the shoulder and ask, "What do you want to be?" You might hear him say, "I wish I had a bunch of lives. I'd like to be a doctor with one of them. I'm crazy about architecture. Also I like farming and animals. I just love my horn; I think I'd enjoy being a band director; and on and on and on . . ."

The elimination of all hallucinatory drugs is highly improbable. The one solution is to diminish their allure. This can only be accomplished by developing young people who find life interesting as it is. There is no other alternative.

****

Jane Flowers is twelve years old. She lives on the East Coast. Obviously a most mature eighth-grader.

"I don't need artificial stimulation. I have plenty of things to do. I like art and making things. I like animals. I like history, home economics, science, swimming, boating, ice skating, I especially like Chester, our dog, and many more things."

ENTHUSIASM

Fun is an important word in the life of a child. It takes many forms but always there is this common ingredient: enthusiasm! "Fun things" beckon for more. There is a quality here of looking forward with promise.

Exactly how a parent can create this magic in a child may vary with the individual.* But it is another mark of our contestants. They do what they do with intensity. They seem to be wringing out the whole experience before they put it aside. The opposite is true of the user. When he talks about turning on, that's exactly what he means. He longs to be recharged.

Chances are this enthusiasm in a child is not so much taught as caught. Question: Is the parent whose ardor has died preparing his son or daughter for drug use?

****

NATURE

Some things are so beautiful they better be left the way they are. When we first read these "Why I Don't Use Drugs" statements, it was as though we were reading from a di-

---

*See PROMISES TO PETER, "interesting things," p. 74.

rectory of worship. So beautifully in touch with life around them. Responsive to nature. Open. Alert. Adding more to their statements would be like putting ruffles on the stars.

"One of the most
treasured gifts
my parents have given me
is the ability to find
beauty and peace in nature,
in city park or
wilderness area.
My foremost hobby is being
an amateur naturalist. This
involves learning the flora,
fauna, and ecology of my
environment and helping
others understand and
appreciate its
uniqueness."

Jody Caudill

"Nature is full of
psychedelic beauty
. . . and sausages
cooking on a grill
smell better than
incense."

Ronnie Paige

"Our
unique vehicle—
body and mind—enables us
to do many things. To look at the
glowing colors of a sunset or a rainbow;
to watch a bird soaring toward heaven
or an insect inching its way across a
rock;
to see with our eyes the smile of a
friend and to feel with our hearts
the warmth and love
being shared."

Peggy Pledger

Exactly how we produce this kind of "turned on" attitude is an elusive study. But it comes in large part from a positive background. In a well-run home there will be some negatives. "Don't," "Stop," "You can't," "I wouldn't" have their place; yet, for the dominant note, these will not do.

"It seems like every meal at our house is 'isn't-it-just-awful' time. Everyone talks about the horrible things on television, and in the papers. Especially, my old man. He doesn't like the government, or his company, or the church, or the weather, or the neighbors. Honest, nothing is any good. You can't trust anything or anyone. Sure, I know drugs can destroy you, but if life's all that bad, what's the difference?"

High school senior

No parent should paint life without some blacks and blues. To overdo the pastels is never honest. But applying the dark colors overmuch isn't fair either. And it might be deadly. Parents do well to check the hope notes around here.

At some stage a young person decides whether life is good. If he decides that it isn't, he is a ripe prospect for trouble. If we can move him to the positive side, we give him good reason to live with purpose.

The "heavy, heavy hangs over thy head" atmosphere is conducive to drug use. Many users suffer from low-grade despair. Some of the despair comes from fear of the future. Anything I can do as a parent to stir up the "Yes" feeling in my child—this is sure to be a good stabilizer.

Tom and Barbara McAllister are a young married couple with two children. He was voted "Outstanding Police Officer" last year in his city. Both are students at a Florida junior college.

"Tom and I are younger than our parents were when they took their diplomas, but we'll be older before we finish. We had our first dates in high school when Tom was too young to even have a driver's permit. His dad chauffeured us. Later, both sets of parents started to get in the way of an early marriage. They knew the statistics. They made sure we knew the odds. But they also trusted us to be responsible. • Tom found work. So we chose to pay now and play later. But we deliberately voted 'no' to drugs. Tom's job and studies make our scene. Having children and growing with them is wonderful. We have experienced a new kind of love through learning together. ***We're high on life, not drugs.***"

III

THE HAPPY, THANK YOU PEOPLE

The nonuser is appreciative

The user feels that life has not done right by him

III THE HAPPY, THANK YOU PEOPLE

Mark Hagen, a Minnesota farm boy, comes from a background of personal struggle. Because of this, his doxology of praise and appreciation takes on special meaning.

"I am sixteen years old and a junior in high school. I live on a farm with my parents and younger brother. Although I now get above average grades, at an early age I found school difficult. I had an emotional problem. I had to go to a speech therapist for help with a speaking disability. Now I am okay on that. Because of my background I have found mental health all important in life. That is why I would never jeopardize my chances of being a whole person by taking any kind of drugs. Through struggle I have learned that happiness and contentment only come from facing reality with courage.
• But there is another reason. My parents have always done the best they could for me. My special education teacher gave me help with my personal problems of which I had so many. Through the patient guidance of all my teachers, my parents' loving care, and the helpful understanding of my classmates, I now enjoy life and hope to continue my education to become a teacher. I am so grateful to the people who helped me that I want to help others up the ladder. This is another reason why I do not take drugs."

Comes now another big difference between user and nonuser. The former is likely to be an injustice collector. He is slanted in the direction of what he doesn't have. He is a complainer. If only he had this one more thing, or two, or six, then he would be grateful.

On the other hand, the nonuser seems slanted in the direction of gratitude. And this is much more than words. He not only knows how to say thank you, he feels it.

Question: What can we do to develop the thankful heart?

Most of us believe that our children should be taught good manners. We like it when people say of our own, "He's a real little gentleman" or "She is a true lady."

But the time must arrive when all this becomes more than words. In the well-rounded personality, appreciation moves one day from "doing" to "being." At their best, manners are a nice part of the inner spirit.

Yet this has to start somewhere. And it better begin early. One sure method is to praise the child when we think he has it coming. Whether it be a little thank you or major, everyone loves a compliment. Anyone who works with the users sees it often—these characters are lonesome for approval.

"Exhibit A" of grateful living between parents is one route to producing gracious people. Children who hear their parents exchanging niceties can more easily express their own feelings of gratitude. By whatever means, we do well to build appreciation into the family philosophy.

One interesting by-road appears often in our entries. Among the things appreciated most by our winners is this: they have been allowed an honest expression of what they don't appreciate.

> "My mom always says, 'the thank you people are the happy ones.' She says it is her aim to make us kids grateful. Only she says we'll never be able to tell how much we like something unless we also feel we can say what we don't like. She says whenever something is bugging us, we should tell her and not somebody else. There aren't many kids whose parents let them do this. So I feel very lucky to have a mother who knows so much about all this. She also says you will get along better when you get married if you know how to say thank you a lot."
>
> From an appreciative junior higher

IV
"I LIKE WHAT I SEE IN THE MIRROR"

The user has
a low
self-estimate
which makes
him
cynical

The
nonuser
has
a healthy
attitude
toward himself

IV "I LIKE WHAT I SEE IN THE MIRROR"

Dig deep enough into the user's thinking and you will find he is running away. Something inside makes him uneasy. He doesn't know what it looks like. But he knows it's there, and his drug is his way of escape.

There are those who deny this. They say, "I do it for kicks" . . . "Don't you see, stupid? Everybody in my crowd does it. It's as simple as that" . . . "Can't you believe? It's because I like it, that's why."

I have met a few whose casual answers seemed for real. But when I came to know them better, the truth held. Something in their unawareness made them need the kicks. Some inner emptiness gave them an excessive longing. An inner craving, unknown but real, had shaped their words, "I like it, that's why."

There is a normal tendency in all of us to project. We blame others. We point the finger away. We look for flaws elsewhere. But true greatness faces in a different direction. It stands at the mirror. It has learned to look itself straight on. This note comes on strong from our entries.

Paul Muongi (second place tie, college senior, New York) sums it up for all:

> "Running away from self only leaves me more exhausted, more accessible to pursuing evils. For me to know the true self is my success. Only then can I know my weaknesses and strengths. Only then can I know the worth of my being."

Few pictures are more thrilling than this: a youth standing at the inner anvil, life before him—shaping, reshaping. And the chances are that he learned this art at home.

Great families do not sit around discussing only the fine things here. They know their assets. They are glad for these. But they also know the weaker stuff which needs some work to make it strong. This does not unnerve them. It serves as a challenge. They can discuss self-analysis openly and unafraid. Which seems somehow to produce this aspect of the nonuser's character. He has a healthy combination of humility and pride.

There is a fine line here. Self-flagellation is not the answer. Society has enough Uriah Heeps already. What we want for our sons and daughters is the calm ability to face facts. And this quality too is more likely caught than taught. We can order them down the hall to the mirror or even drive them there. But they usually learn it best if they see us keeping our paths well worn. Our theme must be:

> "Beginning with mom and dad, home is a laboratory for honest relationships. Let us now sing together, 'Glory be to God for the furnace and the hammer and the file!' "

WARNING

At the same time that we research our weakness we will set up another guard. We will never use scorn. We will refrain from sarcasm. We will eliminate the shaming techniques.

This is a common parental trap. We think that by putting our child down we will encourage him to build himself up. But it never works that way. No matter how clever we may be, this is a fact—demeaning our child in any way makes him vulnerable to the pusher. Anyone with eyes can see how true this is. The user's dress, his walk, his need of a bath all give him away.

Where did he get this poor self-estimate?

Probably at home. And in some cases his low personal opinions came from another sinister error.

"I was brought up on this.
'Don't ever do anything
to make us ashamed, Sue!'
They didn't care anything about
me. All they cared about was
their reputation. So when I
get smashed, I just sit and laugh.
Guess I really gave them something
to be ashamed of,
didn't I?"

College dropout
turned hippie

Certainly we owe a healthy respect to the reputation of the whole. But if we can believe the users, this has lethal results when overdone.

Every family must discover its own routes to honest pride and healthy humility. But however it arrives, these twin qualities come through often from our winners. One high school senior wrote:

"I want to tell you why I wouldn't smoke pot again. I say that, because I did try it for a little while. But then my folks found out about it and they had a talk with me. They were so great. Most parents tell you how ashamed they are. Mine never did. Instead they said I should figure out why I felt like I needed it. So I did, and the reason was mostly because I got put down by someone. Then when I told them about it, they said I was missing a lot by my attitude. What they said was, 'You can learn from things like that if you don't run away from them.' So I decided to think about this, and I began to see a lot of things about myself I didn't know before. I would like to tell everyone that drugs might keep you from learning some things about yourself which could help."

Great parenthood keeps its cool. It does not lash out. It remembers always that people matter more than things—including the family reputation.

THE SOURCE OF GENUINE PRIDE

Another happy surprise waits for those who learn the art of self-analysis. When we turn the spotlights of honesty on ourselves the view isn't all bad. As we uncover our flaws, we discover our strong points. We even find some new reasons to like ourselves. Quiet confidence originates here. So does deep peace.

Training our child to take inventory of his assets and weaknesses produces these things: It gives him a sense of freedom. He is not tied down by the unknown. He can move fast when he needs to. He can move forward, backward, sideways. And he can move far out ahead of the pusher when he knows he should.

Quote from THE STORK IS DEAD correspondence:

"You said I should make a list of all the places where I was trying to kid myself. So I did. It wasn't easy, but I tried to be as honest as I could. Then do you know what happened? All of a sudden I began to see all the neat things about me I didn't know were there."

But this freedom of movement isn't the only good thing we have done. By this training in self-honesty, we make his life interesting. He knows there is a whole psychological zoo behind the scenes. But this doesn't frighten him. He sees it as a challenge. He will slay these, cage those, and make friends with the tamer species.

Another result of honest self-searching seems to be high regard for mental and physical assets.

From our first place winner down, this note sounds clear: Pride is an inside job!

Debrocco Moss (first prize, $500) grew up

in difficult circumstances. But his opinion of himself is more important than the externals:

> "The neighborhood we live in is a poverty condition. There are old houses and weeds and broken glass and beer cans. Trash is found mostly everywhere. But I on the other hand have always been proud of my looks. This is one reason why I do not use drugs. My friends who do are many but they do not look good. They slouch and shuffle and look older than they are. Their eyes droop and they become careless of their person. But I do not want to be sluggish and of poor posture. I want to look the best I can under the circumstances in which I am. This is why I do not use drugs."

Over and over we see it as we work with the young set. The user is more interested in his drug's temporary effect than its long-range damage. He may sense what it is doing to him. So what? He has too little reason to care. Nonusers, on the other hand, have a high sense of pride in body and mind.

Like a steady beat through our entries comes this note. These are proud people, these winners. It isn't braggadocio. It isn't cockiness. They know their limits. Yet they know another thing. They are fully aware of their capabilities. Somewhere they learned a great respect for their assets. They believe in themselves. And they seem to be readying for something worthwhile down the roads of their future.

"I don't use drugs because of the dangers. I would never risk my mind for one quick trip into the unknown, for it might end as an eternity of insanity. If drugs such as LSD were safe, then I feel the experience of hearing a color or feeling a sound would be fantastic. I have found another way—through thinking and dreaming—to see the unknown. The power of the mind is unbelievable when it is used correctly."

Peter Steffens

"I do not want my mind to be beyond my control."

Robin Brown

"I do not
use drugs because
I have a pretty good
mind and I intend
to keep it."

Virginia Leonard

"For our
trip through life,
each of us has been given
a unique vehicle—the human
body. It's more complex than an
Apollo rocket and its controls.
And each of us has been given
the human mind, more intricate than
any sophisticated computer system.
It allows us to find knowledge in
books or from spoken words; to apply
that knowledge for our own growth
and for the benefit of others."

Peggy Pledger

"I am a
senior in high school.
The way I look at it is
this. I have been developing
my mind for eleven years. Why
should I take a chance on
blowing it all now?"

From a straight "A" student

"My first reason for not using drugs is I want to live a healthy life. The drug users I have seen didn't look healthy at all."

Jon Forget

"The brain is the most mysterious organ of the body. It could never be reproduced and patented. So why should I destroy my unique 'computer' that keeps me functioning properly and running smoothly?"

Jeanne Murray

As one high schooler put it: "I like what I see in the mirror. I have a lot of things I want to do. I know I'm not perfect. But I think there are enough strong things in me that I can realize most of my goals."

V

"MY COMMITMENT IS MY DRUG"

The
nonuser
knows the
satisfaction
of
work well done

The user does not
experience
the thrill
of
accomplishment

V "MY COMMITMENT IS MY DRUG"

Paul Muongi
(tie for second, $250)
is the only citizen of
another country to place.
From Nairobi, Kenya,
he came to America and attends
a denominational college in
New York State.
His unusual statement is a sure
pulsebeat of the solid young:
"Challenge and going to meet it
make for excitement."

"Why don't I take drugs? It is difficult to describe all the influences that make a man. But I flash back to my childhood to the days of tending the herd. I was the oldest son, so I was brought to know that I was a man. • As a young boy I had to sleep all night with the sheep and goats. It was a source of pride to know that I was entrusted with the care of the flock. Also, I was given the task of keeping the flock from going astray. Some nights my body would ache with beatings from some man when one of my lambs stole into his garden. Daily I drove the flocks far and wide to look for green pastures. • In spite of fears and hardships, I was proud. My father always encouraged me to be self-confident. He encouraged me to ask the name of strangers and tell them my name. This added to my assurance that I was someone. I won a scholarship to high school in track. In college I prefer cross-country. Every other day I run six miles. Last summer I ran eight miles every day to my summer job. • Since coming to college I am on a new kind of freedom path. I hold close to my heart the teaching by the Apostle Paul, 'Be not conformed to this world, but be ye transformed.' • The person who knows the reason of his being is a committed person, committed to making that life worth living. One who truly commits himself utilizes all his faculties to that commitment. That commitment is his drug. • A committed person is a genuine artist. He loses himself creatively onto canvas to find himself in a finished masterpiece. I have committed myself. In this I am fulfilled. I have no need of any other stimuli."

****

WORK

Next time you meet a fine young person, run a check on his work attitudes. Chances are he came from a home with this philosophy: "Your wishes won't come special delivery tomorrow. Good luck is usually pre-made, and success has a long history."

It is likely also that his work habits were shaped early. Back along the road he has come, you will find him at a job. Somehow he learned how to do things. With his head and his hands, he has experienced the thrill of creating—

a new-mown yard
clean-scrubbed kitchen floor
well-swept patio
snow-shoveled walk
ironing folded

shiny windows
leaves raked
new paint on the fence
fresh-baked cake
table set
beds made

Somebody at some time taught him how to match his wit and his muscles to a challenge.

It is not easy for our children to find jobs outside the home. But is this partially our fault? Would there be more openings had there been more early training?

The wise mother and father will be alert for opportunities. There are numerous little tasks in the family circle. They may not all be creative, but everyone can take his turn on the clean-up squad.

However we do it, this is a fact. The earlier our child can feel any sense of accomplishment, the better. There are drug users who are above-average achievers. But somehow what they accomplished did not satisfy. Why? Perhaps they were never taught to enjoy the little enjoyments.

It is easy to fall down here. So many of the small things are simpler to do ourselves. But from what I've seen, work training should have high priority as we prepare to cope with the drug culture.

One good starting place can be pets. It is surprising the number of winners who made reference to their child–pet relationships. There were so many in fact that we wrote to some of the parents about this. Jody Caudill's parents wrote back that their family has "an ever-changing assortment of pets for which the children have complete responsibility."

Whether it is by the pet route or any other way, this has to be good. Marshaling the child's drives early is valuable experience. At any stage, lessons in how to work pave the road ahead.

RESPONSIBILITY AND SELF-RESPECT

Sheliah Hooks says it for dozens of others:

"I've always had something to be responsible for no matter how small or insignificant it might be, but it was my job to do it, and to do it right."

Sheliah attends a large high school in a major Southwestern city. Having been trained for work, she looks forward to college and a challenging career.

Recognition of himself as a responsible person is one more by-product the child receives from learning how to work. Given something to do and expected to do it, the child gains stature in his own eyes.

A mother in a Family Life Seminar describes it:

> "We think giving your children a sense of pride in themselves is one reason our boys have turned out good, for which we thank God. My husband is an electrician. He began teaching them early about electricity and by the time they were in junior high they could wire a house. Lawrence is making his way through college working for a contractor. Their father would teach them these things and then he would brag to everybody about how smart his boys were. I could see they were embarrassed but I knew they liked it too."

****

MONEY

The well-run family is not likely to be haphazard about money. A carefully planned allowance system goes a long way toward developing maximum maturity. As early as possible a child should have money to spend.

But with it, he should have guidance in how to spend it well. As he becomes more capable, he will appreciate a growing independence. The best rule—allow him to manage whatever he can as fast as he can. In this way he learns to respect the dollar. Even more, he gains prestige in his own eyes.

> "Dad is paid twice a month and I with Ann and Dean write up our needs. Then dad writes a check which covers our needs for two weeks. I have always had this regular allowance which means I have money to spend and budget. Mom and dad have always respected our decisions and they let us use our own judgment."
>
> Jane Flowers

Education at home should include some lessons in true value. We do a good thing when we begin this training early. From every side come many pressures to buy. Always he will need to measure the worth of his dollar against the offered products. The ability to make choices is one more inner stabilizer.

Frequent note in our contest: Drugs are not a good buy!

Palmer Guttromson is a rugged individualist from Dakota. He is a nonuser and he knows why:

"The business men of illegal drugs are, in laboratory analysis, now found to be diluting and selling drugs of low quality. They are selling marijuana diluted by grass clippings and even manure. So are you getting what you buy? • Besides, a 100 to 200 percent profit seems a little high. I work in a lumber yard, hard work. I am not going to be took. • Also, who controls the purity of these kitchen-sink, bathroom-prepared drugs? So, a user plays with death every time he sniffs, drops, or injects. Will the street pushers suddenly repent and not fraud a victim who can't complain? No. • To me, the above reasons are a big factor of doubt to use an illegal drug."

From New York, San Francisco, Omaha, Houston—echoes of the same cool insistence that purchase should be worth its price:

"The person selling drugs cannot guarantee the quality of the goods. He cannot prescribe the adequate dosages nor will he always give one their money's worth."

Ellen Gerowin

"Prices for all drugs available from pushers are much too high. Even if I did have the money I still wouldn't use any form of drug."

Jon Forget

"Since most habit-forming drugs are illegal and are only sold on the black market, the prices are high. This not only causes the user to spend all his money on drugs, but in some cases it causes him to go to extremes. Should I marry, I would not have the time or the money to spend on these drugs and support my family too."

Fred Touchton

"Drugs are a very expensive habit. People who have gotten hooked on drugs may spend fifty dollars per day to support their habit. One pill, the size of a child's aspirin, may cost up to five dollars. After you get hooked on a drug, then you have to buy your drugs. You have to get a job to pay money to buy the drug. It would not be easy to get a job. So you may beg, borrow, or steal the money."

Karen Fedro

"Turning to the practical aspect, being straight certainly does save money. Many of my friends spend 98% of their weekly allowances on grass. They can no longer do the things that they used to love to do with their money for it all goes into drug deals. No more shopping sprees. No more lunches out. No more movies. And they only offer a meaningless excuse when they can't afford to buy their friends any birthday present and their mothers a Mother's Day present. I feel liberated from the financial demands that pressure so many."

Jeannette Bolte

Any way we come to it—

work
the assuming of responsibility
money and the ability to handle it well

—these put young feet on solid footing.

VI

"NEVER SOLVE YOUR PROBLEMS PART WAY"

The nonuser
faces
the hard things
with
courage

The user tends to
fold
when life
goes
against him

VI "NEVER SOLVE YOUR PROBLEMS PART WAY"

"I remember this thing my dad told me. What he said was, 'Never solve your problems part way. You will always be tempted to treat what's on the surface and let it go at that. But smart people get to the bottom of their troubles and solve them there.' It seems to me that my friends who are on dope are doing what my dad said not to do."

A cool high schooler

The user seems to have forgotten this one thing: His "high" can't last! There is no way except to do it again. His escape has a dead end.

Ability to face into the wind is another encouraging character trait of our winners!

Most of us even in adulthood experience fantasy to some degree. We enjoy our delusions. One day we will arrive at our Camelot. No bumps and bruises now. No more disappointment. Everything will be just dandy, thank you!

Some never get over living by mirage. But this is ultradangerous in a drug-prevalent society. One lure of the narcotic is the euphoria it produces. So we have done a fine thing when we teach our children how to deal with the rough times. And it won't be easy. Most of us are overprotective.

We are too quickly invaded by our children's hurt feelings. Yet we must understand that there are places where life demands we go single file. Certain lessons are learned only when we walk the road alone. Life cannot always be idyllic. Success is not finding islands of ease. It is to take the hard things and reshape them. Satisfaction comes by accepting things as they are and molding our own happiness.

Out of our entries a chorus of voices say it over and over:

"Someone offered an escape from the hellish world; but to me it was an escape from one hell into another. It never solved problems, only added more."

Dennis Ballenger

"I like to look at questionable situations as challenges, in which the only possible means of escape is to face and conquer them."

Fred Touchton

"Instead of releasing you from problems, drugs add more to them. Kids help create many of the problems by choosing a destructive way to solve them. Taking drugs adds problems and does not eliminate the original problems. You still have to contend with them."

Tera Tomasina

"My naturalness philosophy by no means guarantees constant happiness. Sometimes I get so terribly down. Instead of spending hours in an unrealistic state of mind, I try to be more constructive. I want to head directly into life and explore it."

Jeannette Bolte

"The problems of the world, or personal problems, can only be coped with face to face. Armies never conquered any nation by constantly retreating."

Lee Darragh

"The users and pushers will say, 'While you are high it is the grooviest and all of your troubles vanish.' They do not tell you the bad part; after the drug wears off, all your troubles return plus a fuzziness of the mind that you had not bargained for."

Virginia Leonard

Question asked often in Parent-Teen workshops: "Should the marijuana law be repealed?"

Answer: No. To legalize pot on the scanty information we have now would not be wise.

There are some good arguments on the other side. It is true many users are able to control their usage. Some contend marijuana is less harmful than alcohol. That may be right. ***But it may be wrong.*** With alcohol we have had long research. Until we are more enlightened, we would be foolish to add another narcotic to the open market.

"The use of marijuana is a felony and when one commits a felony, he loses his right to vote and his right to choose any profession he wishes."

Melissa Thompson

Some of those on the other side honestly feel the whole drug problem could be better controlled if we concentrated on the hard stuff. But there is another reason for keeping it like it is until we understand it better. Thousands of young people have respect for law. They won't take chances with what they know is illegal. In all probability this came out of their early training in the home. Somehow they got the message.

Laws are made for the good of the whole. Some rules of behavior are individual. These may vary from person to person. But the law of the land should only be altered when the majority approves.

> "One of the main reasons I wouldn't is because it's illegal. I know that is the very reason some kids would. I also know this sounds pretty straight but my brothers and I were trained to respect the law. What we were taught is that everybody can't make their own laws or it would be a terrible mess."
>
> High school senior

Note: Threats from parent to child are ineffective. They are also unnecessary. Most young people today are well aware of the penalties:

Guilty of a felony
Lose right to vote
Lose right to own gun
Lose right to run for public office
Can't get a job which requires bonding or license

Can't work for
city
county
federal government

"I have these two friends in my fraternity. They got caught with it in their car. Of course, they were bombed out of school. I just don't feel like it is worth it."

College junior, Texas

Lose opportunity of being
doctor
dentist
pharmacist
realtor
physical therapist
private detective
school teacher
stockbroker
engineer
lawyer
barber
architect
CPA

Can enlist in military service, but will not have choice —probably be assigned to labor battalion.

These facts presented as facts will be enough. Intelligent young minds can work out their own threats.

Rule: Our children's red flags are more effective than ours!

"Ironically many of the 'now' generation are rebelling against the artificiality of our society. Then they turn to artificial forms of mind-searching. But drugs can only provide artificial answers.

"My philosophy of life is that of confronting realism in a positive way, seeing clearly all facets of an issue. Open-minded reasoning is so important in a world of multiple issues.

"Most of my friends use drugs frequently. Drugs of all kinds are readily available. But drugs tend to produce false illusions which in turn build a weak foundation. The drug culture is emphasizing escape. Escape can be no bridge over the world's troubled waters."

Jody Caudill

VII
"WHO WILL HELP AMERICA GROW?"

The user
cares little
for
his country
and the law

The
nonuser
is preparing
himself for
responsible
citizenship

VII "WHO WILL HELP AMERICA GROW?"

It is obvious that some of this generation has grown up with little or no respect for the nation. Why? Have we left too much to the schools? Were we hoping those frequent salutes with classmates would do it? Did we assume that singing "The Star Spangled Banner" before ball games would turn them on to the red, white and blue?

It doesn't. So they move out into the world. One day they meet up with dedicated anarchists. They hear the shouts: "Burn, baby, burn!" . . . "America stinks!" . . . They wonder. This is a new cry. It sounds like destroy!

Sending a child ill-prepared to meet this thrust is unfair . . . unfair to the nation . . . unfair to our sons and daughters.

Of course, there are evils which must be faced by every thinking citizen. We do our children grave injustice when we hide our heads, and theirs, to the truth. But the plain fact is that too few have been trained at home for citizenship. Have we shown them the good things about democracy? If the nation goes down, we will hear the loud shout: "Look what ***they*** did!"

Could it be our fault? Did we fail to educate in freedom? Did we allow our children the right to vote on important matters in the family? Did they learn in our home what it means to respect the other person's opinion?*

A genuine concern for other people—

For every nation
For all races
For world problems

—these require serious education. Early and at home.

Many young lives come up short here. But, thank God, behind the headlines there is another group. There are thousands whose attitudes make the future look good.

Janie Collins, who teaches in a Southern technical school and is also enrolled as a student there, is just one of those who are grateful for their heritage. She is obviously a beautiful person saying some thrilling things about her responsibility to the nation.

---

*See PROMISES TO PETER, "Lessons in Democracy," pp. 78-80.

"For centuries my forefathers struggled to make this country a better place. On the battlefields they fought to establish and preserve our rights. Should I ignore their contribution? Should I shrug my shoulders and say, 'So what?' • The world today needs people like me who are willing to continue trying to improve America's greatness by being the type citizen who can support himself and his family and contribute to those who are less capable mentally and physically.

• I don't smoke pot because many giants in my memory are challenging me to live a purposeful life."

Another Jane says it her way:

> "In a few years young people will control and protect our country. If lots of kids get a hangup for drugs, who will help America grow and build her strength? This world is ready to help me if I will help myself to become more capable of filling the shoes of the leaders who leave their positions to my generation."
>
> Jane Flowers, age 12

Those who suffer from a waning hope will be glad to know there are many more of this same conviction. Numberless young people still salute the flag with meaning. And plenty among them are "willing to continue trying to improve America's greatness."

"I am in the process of making myself and the world more perfect without the help of drugs."

Robin Brown

"The future of the world lies in our hands; the hands of the young people. To take this great responsibility, our hands must be steady."

Virginia Leonard

"Since I am not running from reality, I can take effective steps to insure a better world. I have a responsibility to see that my children will grow up in a world more peaceful, more beautiful than the world in which I am now growing up."

Clark Jobe

CONCERN FOR OTHERS

What makes the difference between the rabble rouser and the genuinely concerned? I suspect the answer flashes back to the child's own sense of worth. We have seen that these young people have a strong self-image. If theirs is a healthy sense of merit, concern does not stop here. The other person is good for something too. This rare quality of mind is one of the greatest gifts we can give a child. There is room in his world for all kinds of people. Some of them can do what he cannot. So? He has no need to be jealous. He will contribute his part. Others will contribute theirs. And all together the world shapes up.

This is the basis of social concern. The young person who believes that others have worth cares about their chances.

In all honesty, most adults would have to admit it. The crowd we grew up with wasn't disturbed about poverty. We accepted the poor as part of the scenery. We weren't bothered about desecrating the earth. Most of us hadn't even heard, let alone cared about, ecology. Pollution in our air, filth in our rivers—these scarcely warranted thought one from us. We had important things to do.

Thank God this is no longer true. Today's young thinker is drawing the circle larger. His is a broader concept of citizenship. His liberties are only safe when they are extended to everyone. He has no more right to his rights than anyone else on earth. At his best he cares about the hungry child behind that empty tin cup. Selling a war to today's young gets harder by the hour.

What shapes these minds in this direction? Some of them get that way from new influences as they near adulthood. Maybe we should be grateful any time a son or daughter is turned on to the needs of others. But some of this awakening seems headed for trouble. There are sane and insane ways to rebuild society. And the difference, from reading my mail, comes clear. The safest revolutionist is one who was shaped that way early against a loving background. I get the distinct impression that the creation of a finer tomorrow for all men waits on a generation which is trained at home.

That's what they tell me.

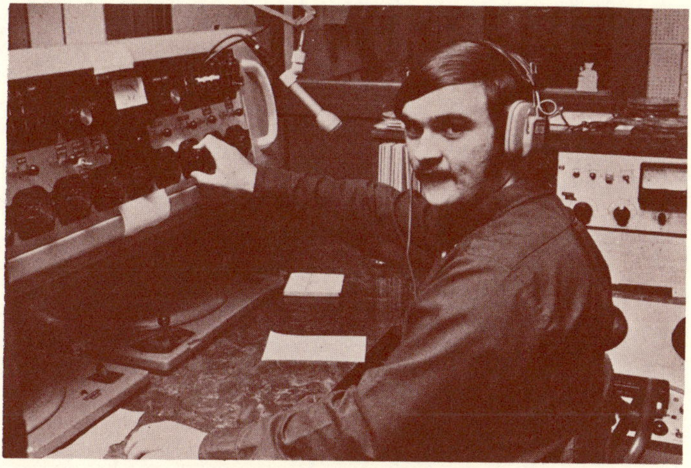

Larry Barber is a sophomore in a large Southwestern university. He is majoring in communications—radio, television, journalism.

"Man has many responsibilities, but his greatest are tnose to himself and others. To fulfill his obligations, the responsible person tries to function to his maximum capabilities to reshape the world. He strains to hear the cries of the helpless, strives to understand the problems of others, and works to alleviate pain. • The responsible person protects his body and mind so that he can correctly interpret problems and seek their answer. The 'tripper' is no help to himself or others. Drugs blind the eyes, deafen the ears, cloud the mind. Important things are minimized; the unimportant becomes important. • A united struggle of all people would bring a better world. I was taught to love people and I want to help. The responsible person rolls up his sleeves to solve problems. • That is why I do not use drugs."

VIII

"IF YOU COULD SEE MY MOM AND DAD"

The nonuser respects his sexuality, so he is not afraid to be male or female

The user is sexually immature, making him confused about his role

VIII "IF YOU COULD SEE MY MOM AND DAD"

One trait of the winners is a healthy respect for their sexuality.

Prior to writing THE STORK IS DEAD, I authored a column in TEEN magazine on sex and dating. I have talked to and heard from thousands of teens about their sex problems.* I am increasingly amazed at their maturity.

---

*Editor's Note: For fuller treatment of this subject, see Charlie W. Shedd, THE STORK IS DEAD (Waco, Texas: Word Books, 1968). Discussion in IS YOUR FAMILY TURNED ON? is purposely limited to avoid repetition.

THE STORK IS DEAD, an immediate bestseller, grew out of dialogue and correspondence with more than twenty thousand teenagers. Written for teenagers in language they can understand and believe, this continues to be the frankest book on the market on teenage sex problems. And not only teenagers, but parents, medical doctors, educators, ministers, and psychologists are enthusiastic in acclaiming it the most helpful and useful book of its kind to date. FWT

Sure, there are the otherwise—confused, in trouble, or about to be. But most of them are more open, more honest, more wholesome than our generation.

To borrow one of their own terms, what they want is "the straight skinny." Given this, the majority will shape their own healthy attitudes.

Preaching they do not need, nor moralizing. Neither are they moved by scare tactics. This is one more place where threats will not work. The waving of danger flags doesn't seem to affect them. By the teen years, they have their own inner tribunal. The average youth today can see clearly how not to. He and his friends know that babies come from intercourse. And is there any community without its exhibit of this negative?

Yet the whole thing is much more subtle than unwanted pregnancies. Up and down the halls, in locker room and over the phone, at parties—wherever the gang gathers, they hear these more subtle things. In their friends' faces, they see them. Inside their own souls they feel them. The reading they get tells them clearly: what's wrong with sex is largely what isn't right!

So most young people, with adequate help, can figure it out. Given the whole truth in the right way, at the right time, they'll handle sex right. And if you could read my mail, you'd get it loud and clear. ***The right setting for sex information is a turned-on home—turned on to love in all its facets!*** I see it again and again. Generally, sex attitudes at their best have one common origin. They are the product of a family where sex was faced, and discussed, and appreciated.

Question: What constitutes effective sex education in the home?

Four answers:

1. ***Demonstration.*** At our house is love between male and female beautiful? From watching us, can our children sense a good thing? Are we showing them that sex is a means of grace rather than a source of guilt?

> Two witnesses describe it for us:
>
> "If you could see my mom and dad and how they love each other, you would know why I want a marriage just like theirs."
>
> "My parents were divorced when I was small, but I admire the way my mother has done. She has told us why their marriage didn't work and even what she thought she did wrong. And I never once heard her run my father down. She has

> taught us children that love should be beautiful and she has told us that we should look forward to the kind of home we didn't have. From talking to my friends whose parents are divorced, I think she is very unusual."

2. ***Early verbalizing is a must.*** To wait till the teen years is a serious mistake. By the time he arrives here, the teenager has a fierce drive to belong. There is a screaming inside him for approval. He is threshing about for identity. Because this is true, he needs adequate pre-thought on sex. Every confusion we can eliminate better prepares our child to cope with the drug culture.

> "I don't remember when it began, but it seemed as if we always discussed sex like it was very natural. My dad took me with him a lot and when it was time, he told me what he wanted me to know. Then he asked me if there was anything I wondered about. So I asked him some stuff and now whenever I wonder, I go talk with him. It is so great the way all my friends come to both my mom and dad for whatever they don't understand."

3. ***Education for independent thinking.*** We do well to teach our children early how to make their own decisions, determine their own

values, stick to their beliefs in the face of pressures. This is another part of good sex education.

> "My mother has ***always*** taught me to be independent, to think for myself; do something because I want to, not because everybody else is doing it."
>
> Sheliah Hooks

4. ***Reverence.*** Running through our entries is a near devotional attitude toward their sexual future. As we have noted most of this originates in the home. We have also observed that they have seen plenty on the other side of good. From these two sources, there comes a sense of respect for great sex. These young people are not "squares." They are vibrant with emotional response. But somewhere they came to this realization: Many things are greater if their greatness is reserved for the right time.

Debrocco Moss is one of these.

Our first prize winner, he lives in the ghetto of a large city. Several things in his original entry caught the eye of the judges. One of these was his statement that some of his friends were "getting their sex messed up by drugs." When asked to enlarge on this theme, he did. Edited from ten pages of vivid description, here is his classic statement.

Debrocco Moss,
first place winner

Sex Life in the Ghetto

"A boy is worried about bills, problems of his community, home and school. He likes to get rid of it all. His friends are going to a drug abuse and sexual party. He accepts his friends' offer. • The party really comes to life when some of the boys start going into the rooms with girls. Most of these girls have venereal disease. Everyone has been smoking marijuana. He takes the drug and tells his friend he feels really superior. So he does his thing with the girls. • Three days later he has venereal disease and it is greatly affecting him. To get relief he goes to another drug party. Several days later he is again in great pain. To get money for more drugs he tries stealing or borrowing. Next he is caught by the police and locked up in jail in great pain. • So how can he be cured now? And if he isn't cured, this may affect his sexual organs where he may not be able to use them. There is big trouble for him for he may not even be reproductive to a woman. I have known some others where drugs have caused them to commit a rape which this person may never have committed in his life. So everything you wished for or dreamed about may come down. What started all this? Drugs are what started it. I know this for truth because I have some friends to whom this has happened. • But that is not all. Drugs have caused persons to use themselves wrong. There may be homosexuals at that party. If you do everything they tell you for fun this may lead to the experience of homosexuality. • This transfer is wrong. God has made man for woman and woman for man. And a man should be a man and a woman a woman. • This, as I already said, was caused under the influence of certain drugs. You may check this in a book but I know for truth because I also know persons for whom this thing has happened too. • So some people may think they are on Cloud Nine when using drugs, but they don't know that Cloud Nine may be taking them for a farewell ride. All this is one more reason why I do not use drugs, and it is because I respect my sex."

IX
"MY THING IS TO NOT DO YOUR THING"

The nonuser has been encouraged to use his own judgment, giving him a healthy independence

The user struggles to be free, and his feelings of repression make him hostile

IX "MY THING IS TO NOT DO YOUR THING"

"What gets me
is how inconsistent my
friends are when they are getting
high. They say, 'Come on, Jerry,
do your thing.' Sometimes they
even get nasty. So I just say,
'Can't you see, stupid?
My thing is
to not do
your thing?' "

High school sophomore

"I get
so turned off
the way they
tell me. 'You
have the guts to
turn on.' This
really bugs me.
I think it is exactly
the opposite. You
have the guts
not to."

South Carolina
high school sophomore

Word from wise parents:

"We really shouldn't blame the kids for wanting everybody's approval. Without meaning to do it, we taught them by inference to care too much what others think. I mean we got too excited when somebody criticized us. In other words, we cared too much, so they do too."

"My parents let me do things by myself and they trust me."

Steve Bartholomew

"I have always been allowed to make my own decisions and formulate my own values."

Patricia Popham

"My parents have continually encouraged creative education and free thinking."

Jody Caudill

"Doing my thing" is a phrase with great meaning for today's teenager. But the pity is that so many young people are confused here. They will gladly raise a fuss for the right to do their own thing. Yet many do not know what their thing is.

This is not true of our winners. These young people have been trained for independence. They have been educated for it at home.

From a recent Parent-Teen Seminar, this word:

> "We think one of the most important things is to train our children respect for their own judgment. We do this by allowing them to make as many decisions for themselves as they are capable of making. Sometimes they will even say, 'I wish you would decide for me.' Maybe we will, if it doesn't matter much. But then again, we may say, 'No! Some day you're going to have to think for yourself. This is a good time to begin.' It is hard to know exactly how much of this is enough, but we think it is very important."

It is. By the teen years most young people are largely doing their own thinking anyway. As parents, we have finished our sanding and polishing. Not much left to do now but relax and enjoy the product.

It is a fortunate child who grows up in a home with this philosophy:

> "Each of us here is a unique individual. Our job is not to fence each other in. It is to help each person become his best self."

In the wise home there are plans for the achievement of self-government. The goal should be for each member to be handling his own control wherever he can as rapidly as he can.*

PREPARATION FOR DRUGS: THE HOSTILITY BUILD-UP

Question: Where does all this fit into the drug scene?

Answer: At one all-important, ultracrucial point: ***The child who is allowed to think for himself is less likely to be wasting his energies with hostility!***

---

*PROMISES TO PETER, Section I, "A Growing Self-Government," outlines in detail a schedule toward which each child moves. The philosophy is: "The more I let my child think for himself, the more he will care what I think."

Anyone who talks much to the user knows this is a common part of the drug base. Like a broken record:

"I had this smart sister, see? I mean, this kid was a brain. So all the teachers said, 'Why don't you be like Sharon?' So I tried. God, how I tried. Then one day I said to myself, 'Annie, girl, this isn't your bag!' So I just gave up and came out here, and now look at me. So maybe I don't like it, but at least nobody is asking me why I don't be like Sharon."

West Coast teenager on drugs

From an addict,
college junior:

"My old man is a chemistry professor. So he has this big thing about me making some wild discovery. Crazy, man! Like it would be some real big deal. So all I care about is art and he thinks that's stupid. So nothing I could ever do would satisfy him. So, what the hell!"

In direct contrast to these attitudes our winners' resentment is long gone. Their inner atmosphere is free from rancor. These are happy people. They seem possessed of genuine joy at being alive.

Anyone interested in planting a song in his child's heart will be asking: "How do they get this way?"

One answer comes clear. The secret is not to repress anger, but to surface it intelligently.

The healthiest young people are those who have had some blowing-off points. Naturally the safest place for these hostility vents is at home. When they are ugly with us, sometimes we should let it pass. Perhaps today it took all the good in them to monitor their public behavior. In the teen years it is well to provide them some place for their groaning.

****

THE BURIED SELF AND THE YEARNING TO BELONG

The authoritarian home may be doing another bad thing.

> "I would give anything I have, and I do mean anything, if I could show somebody exactly what I am like."
>
> Lonesome at Seventeen

Why? Somewhere she got locked in. And one sure place this happens is a particular kind of home. Without anger vents, not permitted to express her dislikes, she doesn't express anything. She clams up. Which, as the teen world knows, is not unusual.

Neither is the desire to be known unusual. Every human being comes ready-built with this inner longing. As one girl put it, "I feel like we are playing hide and seek, and I am the one who is hiding. Only nobody is seeking me!" So, where did she start hiding? Probably very early in the family interchange, or lack of it. One day she put up some protective walls to keep from being hurt. Then she built them higher. Thicker.

Some of the bizarre on the youth scene is nothing more than the frantic search for a way out.

Say it one more time. In the home successfully coping with the drug culture, there will be some safety valves!

But there is a very important key here. This is the one which unlocks the door for communicating the negative. And the label is ***mercy!*** Judgment, derision, moralizing—these must go. We are most likely to surface our real feelings only when we are certain they will be received in love.

Note: Undisciplined blow-up is not the answer. Every home needs limits. But it also needs these things as part of its basic philosophy:

(a) the child's right to express his dislikes
(b) some training in how to do it with dignity

DIALOGUE FROM A HIGH SCHOOL YOUTH GROUP:

"Why do you think most of them do it?"

"The ones I know who go on grass and stuff have something against someone."

"Like who?"

"Like the whole world maybe and especially their folks."

"Didn't you ever hate your parents?"

"Sure. Only with me it didn't last."

"Why didn't it last?"

"Well, I think it is because they told me it was all right to feel that way. You know, like it's no big thing. They even told me to get it off my chest if I didn't like something."

"How did they recommend you do that?"

"Well, just saying how I felt. Like if I didn't think they were being fair, they said I should tell them. So I did. Of course I had to do it right. But when I did they would listen. They really would."

"Then what did they do?"

"Oh, sometimes they would change things. But if they didn't, they would explain why they felt like they did. I think that's important. So many parents won't give a kid a chance."

Is Your Family Turned On?

"What do you think makes parents so different?"

"Well, I don't exactly know only I think it is kind of like this. Some parents think they are God and I feel sorry for my friends whose folks are like that. Then there are parents like mine who tell me, 'The most important thing is for you to decide what God wants you to do.' I guess of all the things I like about my mom and dad, this is what I like best."

X

"THIS CAT WAS TOGETHER, MAN"

The nonuser feels responsible to God and he is grateful to Him

The user suffers from chronic despair, because he has little faith in anything

X "THIS CAT WAS TOGETHER, MAN"

In Pittsburgh there is an interesting youth show called THE PLACE. It is held in a large television studio, attractively set up like an Italian restaurant. Checkered red and white cloths on the small tables give it atmosphere. Candles in wine bottles provide most of the light. Some "now" music keeps the joint jumping. The guest leader for the day sits on a raised dais in the middle of the room.

The show is run by the young set. They invite whoever they want, and this day it was my turn.

I will never forget the opening comment. It came from a college freshman. I liked him. Nice sort. Obviously new on the mod scene. Big glasses. Large. Round. Pink. His hair was long and you could tell he was proud of what little beard he had managed to grow.

Out of deep-set eyes he looked at me. Then he said this thing which wrote itself on my heart:

> "If you want to talk to me about your church, dad, drop dead. I got no use for the church. But if you want to talk to me about Jesus, that's something else. We can rap about him a long time. This cat was together, man."

Somehow he gathers the feelings of many in his age group. Being a churchman, I'm sorry about the decline in respect for the church. But we better believe it. By the thousands they are turning us off. Denominations, things ecclesiastical, formal worship, organized religion are all a part of "the God squad." And "the God squad" has had it with this crowd.

> "I am not a churchgoer, yet I feel closer to the Spirit than my acquaintances."
>
> Palmer Guttromson

But they are not irreligious.

Where did they lose the "Sunday-morning-we-all-get-dressed-and-go-to-church" feeling? Here are some answers right out of their bull sessions.

"The last time I went to church, our preacher told all about why we need a new organ. It cost a lot. That same week I started working at Head Start. Would you believe that there are kids in our town who don't have decent clothes for school? So I went to talk to our preacher about it. What he said was, the government should take care of people like that. I happen to know that is not the teaching of Jesus."

North Carolina
college freshman

"The thing is I think the church is completely irrelevant. They just aren't doing anything that matters any more."

College youth,
Billings, Montana

"The church just doesn't make any difference. My folks go all the time, but they don't live up to it. The preacher preaches one thing and they do another."

High schooler, Austin, Texas

Sure there are some outstanding exceptions to these indictments, but the sounding from the heads and hearts of these young people comes on strong. They are not "churchy." Yet they have deep religious feelings.

Third place winner
Clark Jobe, age 15

"The church has not carried a profound influence. As a child, I attended the Methodist church. As I reached adolescence, my mother, exercising her great wisdom, afforded me the choice of remaining within the church or finding another more to my liking. I, like many other teenagers, have 'establishmentitis.' I had seen the staunch, conservative Western church. So I set out with the winds of change billowing my sails. I accepted a new set of postulates. I have turned inward to find a church. Call it what you will, it's there!"

Questions: When should parents turn their children loose to decide for themselves about formal religion? When should worship be optional?

Some parents contend that from infancy up, children should be completely unprejudiced. These hold that the child should never be made to worship or attend church school. "I want my children to decide for themselves which religion to follow. When they're old enough, they can make this decision."

There is one major flaw in this kind of thinking. The little mind abhors a vacuum. Something will make its way in to guide and control.

From reading our winning entries the evidence stands firm. One strong shaper of the early character was religious training in the church. Some are still loyal to their tradition. But even these give us the feeling they are still loyal because *they* choose to be.

> "The greatest thing my parents did was to introduce me to God. I attended services as a child. But once they made the introductions, mom and dad left the rest up to God and me. Happily, we've been the best of friends ever since—something I don't think would be true if it had been demanded of me."
>
> Becky Bavin

Conclusion—

Vital religion is an inside job!

Therefore, one more goal of my parenthood is to help my child shape his own religion. But I cannot do this by words alone. Plastic sainthood is no longer effective. Today's young mind is too sharp for religion which is only facade. It is amazing how many users come from super-pious homes. I must show by my own living what life with the Inner Presence can be! In a drug-prevalent society, a strong inner Center of Reference is a tremendous stabilizer. I can tell my child about it. I can take him where others will do the same. But this too is evident: It is more likely to be meaningful if he first sees it demonstrated.

****

THE JOY OF THE LORD

What will the religion of tomorrow be like?

Nobody knows for sure. But from what I've seen, some things are plain. If orthodoxy means being gloomy about God, this crowd will gladly be called heretics. ***Worship for turning them on must sound the high notes of celebration.***

Tuning in to their complaints against us, listening for the sound of truth in their numerous

charges, trying hard not to be defensive—
this note I hear like a broken record:

"You want to know
why I quit?
Well, I'll tell you. All
I ever heard about was sin
and how bad we all are.
Now I don't mind some of that.
I know we're bad.
But is that
all we are?"

"You guys won't
believe this, but one
time I was on the youth
ushers. You know what I
found out? I found out they
even got rheostats for keeping it
dark. I guess why I quit was I was
afraid one Sunday I would stand up
and holler, 'For Christ's sake
turn on the lights!' "

Do you suppose it's possible these young "turners-off" of the church are doing mankind a favor? It could be, if out of this time in history we wake up to the truth. Religion at its finest ***is*** a celebration. It is a life-song in praise to the God who loves us, a response to the Lord who means us to live in a natural high with him.

Patricia Popham sounds the note:

"Many of my generation put God in the bottom drawer. This is a personal thing and I try not to criticize those who feel religion isn't their bag. But it is real for me. I feel the need to take what He gave me and celebrate life. This is my religion. I can honestly say to Him, 'Thank you for giving me every hour of every day.' "

CLOSING SOUNDS

CLOSING SOUNDS

"Isn't it awful? They're coming from the best homes!"

This we hear often and it is sometimes true. Nobody knows for sure who's next. The parent who says, "My child would never," may be whistling past the graveyard. It is much wiser to stay on the alert.

It will be immediately apparent that our term "best homes" needs defining. We have a way of assuming that two cars and a swimming pool automatically qualify for "best." But sometimes homes we wouldn't consider "half-best" produce great character. Which means in part that it isn't how much we have. It's how we have what we have that counts.

Those in the know on the drug scene will readily admit it—we don't know enough to judge. I find no variance among the experts. One hundred percent of them disclaim any expertise. There are simply too many unknowns here. Too many handles we thought we had break off in our hands. There are too many side roads of the emotions and too many by-paths of the mind. Too many influences, conscious and unconscious, warn us against glib answers.

Even when we're ninety percent sure, there is a fuzzy ten percent of total mystery. For this reason it is always best to be tentative about our conclusions. So one of our guidelines can well be a kind tongue.

Gentleness! Sympathy! Understanding! These are most likely to be the sounds of those who have been around much in this strange country.

And they should be the closing sounds of any discussion from the drug scene.

A PERSONAL MESSAGE TO YOU . . . THE READER

It is quite likely that no other writer in America today is as widely read and accepted by both teenagers and parents as Dr. Charlie Shedd. He writes to be read . . . and he is!

PROMISES TO PETER, published in 1970, talks about building bridges from parents to children. In a very real sense, it is a handbook for IS YOUR FAMILY TURNED ON?.

PROMISES TO PETER is a "how to" book on happy relationships and relaxed communication within the family—between husband and wife, parents and children. Of the several promises made to Peter on the day of his birth, Charlie Shedd selects three as all-important: for ***Growing Self-government,*** to give ***Lessons in How to Love,*** and to teach and demonstrate the ***Dignity of Work.***

Here are revolutionary ways for parents and children to "do their thing"—to be happy in the doing, and to find authenticity as persons in the art of creative family living.

This is what a few of the readers have said about it:

HERE IS CHILD PSYCHOLOGY ENCOUCHED IN THE MOST PRACTICAL APPLICATIONS. . . . READ THIS ONE TO ENJOY—BUT READ ALSO TO LEARN.

Sacramento Bee

THIS BOOK BUILDS A BRIDGE FROM PARENT TO CHILD IN DISCUSSING SELF-GOVERNMENT, HOW TO LOVE, AND THE DIGNITY OF WORK. A MAGNIFICENT BOOK TO GIVE OR TO CHERISH.

The Baptist Sunday School Board

AN INFORMAL CHATTY BOOK OF WHOLESOME FAMILY WISDOM.

The Los Angeles Times

YOU'LL FIND THIS BOOK A FRESH, GIVE-AND-TAKE LOOK AT THE INGREDIENTS NECESSARY FOR A FULL, RICH FAMILY LIFE AND WHAT EACH MEMBER OF THE FAMILY MUST PITCH INTO THE POT.

American Lutheran Reading Club

READING "PROMISES TO PETER" COULD HELP YOUR CHILDREN TO HAVE MORE UNDERSTANDING PARENTS.

Atlantic Baptist

CHARLIE SHEDD WRITES WITH UNDERSTANDING AND UNFAILING GOOD HUMOR; SOME OF THE INSIGHTS THAT EMERGE SHOULD PROVE TO BE POINTERS FOR PARENTS.

Presbyterian Life

THERE IS A RICH MINE OF WISDOM AND INSPIRATION FOR PARENTS HERE.

Together

"PROMISES TO PETER" IS A BOOK RECOMMENDED FOR ANY PARENT LOOKING FOR HAPPINESS IN THE HOME AND WHO DESIRES TO KEEP THE FAMILY TOGETHER. IT IS RECOMMENDED FOR CHILDREN WHO WANT TO KNOW WHAT IT IS LIKE TO LIVE IN A HOME THAT IS REAL. THE AUTHOR USES A LOT OF IMAGINATION, IS CREATIVE, AND LEAVES THE READER SPELLBOUND.

The Jackson Sun

We know you will agree!

****

THE STORK IS DEAD, also by Dr. Charlie Shedd, grew out of a dialogue through correspondence with almost 20,000 teenagers . . . readers of his columns in *Teen* magazine on sex and dating. This is the frankest book on sex yet, written for teenagers in a language they can understand and believe. What it says has been applied and proven—it works.

He was a typical young American; sharp, natural, straightforward. He wrote: ***I don't care whether it's wrong. I want to know whether it's smart. Now don't give me your old religious pitch. I'm looking for some adult who will cool his moral fever long enough to tell me what's smart for me.***

Teenagers want straight answers to honest questions on sex, and Dr. Charlie Shedd pulls no punches.

These agree:

This book serves a real need, both for young people who seek to understand themselves and the opposite sex better and for the parents who are trying to help them toward such an understanding. The stork is dead, but thankfully Charlie Shedd is alive and talking turkey.

The Houston Post

Shedd is extremely frank, which is something teenagers respect a great deal in adults, and he also puts sexuality in a very positive Christian context.

Eternity

Dr. Shedd's approach is articulate, informed, and totally without the hypocrisy the young people so deplore. As with his previous books, "Letters to Karen" and "Letters to Philip," this new one will do a lot of good if the right young people find it in time.

The Denver Post

There is no doubt in my mind that this is the best book I've ever read on the subject of sex put in teenage language. I wish every teen would read this book . . . [it] gets the message over to teenagers.

Reviewer for Standard Publishing Company

"The Stork Is Dead" could be a great ice breaker for families who have difficulty communicating, especially if the parents read it as well as the teenagers.

The Nashville Tennessean

If you are looking for a Scripturally oriented source which can be a frame for conversations between parents and teenagers, this can be a valuable reference.

Christian Home and School

It is hoped that this book will also be read by parents and discussed with their children. The first vital condition in understanding is communication. Healthy communication, free from fear of criticism and/or guilt would certainly help breach the generation gap.

American-Statesman (Austin, Texas)

This is a book we all have needed for a long time. It separates "sex" from the meaningful experience of married love, and there's a lot of difference. It communicates to the young and old alike, and believe me, there are lots of married people that can improve their relationship by reading this book.

Eugene H. Arrendell, M.D. (Ponca City, Okla.)

A book I want my children to read—and written so they will. Straight . . . solid.

Charles T. Frey, M.D. (Cedaredge, Colo.)

****

Both ***Promises to Peter*** and ***The Stork Is Dead*** discuss principles and concepts that can revolutionize home and family life. We urge you to read them for that reason. They should be available in the book or department store which you patronize regularly; however, if you experience any difficulty in locating them, please write us.

The Publisher